Making Mortgage Sense

Ron Culver

AisA, LLC—Bozeman, MT
ISBN: 979-8-218-20590-4
Library of Congress Control Number: 2023910160
Title: *Making Mortgage Sense*
Author: Ron Culver
Digital distribution | 2023
Paperback | 2023

Table of Contents

Introduction

Throughout my life, I've heard the phrase, "Buying a home is the biggest financial transaction of a person's life," uttered more times than I can count. It's probably true for 99.9% of the people in the world, but what those words of wisdom do not adequately convey is that it's also one of the most stressful transactions of a person's life. We are talking about a home … a place where friends and family gather: the place where kids are raised and pets are cuddled; the place where you sleep and you most want to feel safe. There is a lot of emotion involved. As someone sitting on the "customer" side of the loan officer's desk, one must also deal with a strange process that is a massive invasion into your personal private information and seems to go on forever. Emotion does not pair well with business transactions. It's even worse when you don't have a clue what is going on or can't understand why it is that the loan officer is asking for so much information. So, I hope to change all that with what you're about to read.

You will be taken on a journey that encompasses the manufacturing of a mortgage loan. Make no mistake—it *is* a manufacturing process, a lot like an assembly line for an automobile. But, instead of line workers bolting on fenders, doors, wheels and engines, you will have loan officers, processors, underwriters, closers, funders and many more behind-the-scenes professionals who will assemble a bunch of parts to complete this widget called a "mortgage loan." Just like a vehicle that rolls off the assembly line and is sold to a happy new customer, a mortgage loan is often sold to a happy new investor after it is "built." And, yes, investors *are* happy to purchase your mortgage loan because they become the recipients of a mortgage payment every month for many years. Your loan and the right to receive payments on it (called "mortgage servicing rights"—more on that later) are commodities to be bought and sold just like frozen concentrate orange juice, coffee, or cocoa beans.

There are different business models in mortgage lending: Banks, non-banks (also called "independent mortgage banks" or "IMBs") and mortgage brokers. They all have their merits and, despite being different models, they all follow the same basic process. We'll briefly discuss each of the three so that you will understand them. However, regardless of which path you choose, what you learn from this book will apply to each.

So—buckle up, grab some popcorn and your favorite beverage and be prepared to be the most well-educated among your non-mortgage professional friends on the ins and outs of mortgage lending.

Chapter One
To bank or not to bank—Is that really even a question?

If you were to ask a member of the Greatest Generation where you should go to get a loan to buy a home, they would probably tell you to go to a bank. It makes sense: Banks have money to lend. That's the way it has been for generations and the conventional wisdom applies even today. However, we have more options now, largely due—at least in part—to the concept of capital markets. To understand this better, we must embark on a brief history lesson.

Capital markets

Before the idea of capital markets, banks and savings institutions were responsible for most lending—not just mortgage lending but all kinds. You want to buy a car? Get a loan from the bank. You want to start a business and need capital? Ask your local banker. You want to purchase [insert the object of your desire here] but don't have the cash to pay for it? Get a loan from the bank. That is all well and good until the bank you patronize does not have money to lend. "Banks without money to lend, you say?" Yeah, it can happen. Banks lend out the money they have on deposit from their customers. These customers stash their cash in banks in many forms. It could be a checking or savings account, or maybe a Certificate of Deposit. Regardless of the instrument or product on behalf of whom the money is deposited, the bank has your money and keeps it safe and sound through its financial security and maybe a little help from the Federal Deposit Insurance Company (FDIC). Each time you check your account balance to see if you have enough to pay for that venti quad-shot maple pumpkin spice latte, you see a balance that appears to be sitting idle since the last time you swiped your debit card. However, this is somewhat of an optical illusion. Banks (or other depositories) use your money like crazy when you're not. On average, they tend to loan out $0.80 to $0.90 for every dollar they have on deposit. The ratio of loans compared with deposits is called the "loan-to-deposit ratio." As a practical example, if Charlotte deposits $10.00 with her bank in Miramar, the bank may loan out $8.50 of that to Pete so that he can buy his motorcycle. If that were the entirety of the deposit and lending portfolio of that bank, this would be an 85% loan-to-deposit ratio as calculated by $8.50 ÷ $10.00 = .85 or 85%.

Now, back to the idea of a bank not having money to lend. If the institution in question has established that they will not exceed an 85% loan-to-deposit ratio, then they can no longer make loans once that ratio is reached. Before further loans can be made, they will need to either get more money on deposit or have existing loans paid off. In the very unique circumstance whereby a town has only one bank and that bank has reached its lending limit, a consumer may have no opportunity to borrow money (except, maybe, from Uncle Scrooge, but his terms are terrible!). This is where capital markets enter the story. Think of capital markets as a social club where mortgage lenders and fat cats from Wall Street with money burning holes in their pockets get together for drinks. The lenders talk to the investors about a customer of theirs (let's call her "Marge") looking to buy a home at 742 Evergreen Terrace. They discuss things like her credit worthiness, income and assets and the condition of the home. If the details of the loan package sound good to the investor(s), they will make an offer to purchase the loan once it closes. You've probably heard of social networking? This is like "financial networking" where lenders meet investors who want to lend money and/or buy loans, thereby facilitating the flow of capital from Wall Street to Main Street.

Capital markets ultimately changed the landscape of mortgage lending by allowing institutions other than banks (like IMBs) to make mortgage loans to essentially anyone who qualifies, not just a bank customer. This also allows banks to provide mortgage loans to consumers without having an impact on their loan-to-deposit ratios because they can sell the completed loans to the investors, which keeps them off their lending portfolios.

An IMB will generally work with a number of different investors (via the social club) and make available to consumers all the different loan products (more on those later) that those investors offer. There are a large number of IMBs for the average consumer to choose from. If you're working with a loan officer and you're not sure of the business model their company follows, it is easy to tell: If you can deposit money with their institution, they are probably some form of depository institution (such as a bank or credit union). If they don't take deposits but will take your mortgage application, underwrite it and close it, they are probably an IMB. If they don't take deposits and have someone else underwrite and close your loan after you've given them an application, they are probably a mortgage broker (more on them soon). For an entrepreneur looking to get into mortgage lending, an IMB or a mortgage broker is a good business model for them if they are unable to open their own bank.

A mortgage broker is the third major business model in the mortgage world next to banks and IMBs. Such brokers work with wholesale lending banks to offer loans to consumers. They collect an application and supporting documentation (used to verify, for example, income, assets and employment) from a consumer and send them to a wholesale bank so that a lending decision can be made. Then, once the loan closes, they collect a payment from the wholesale bank for bringing them a customer. They operate similar to an auto insurance broker. With auto insurance, you can go directly to a big insurance company (like the ones you see on TV commercials) to get your comprehensive and collision insurance or you can go to an insurance broker. That broker will collect information about you, your driving record and that sweet ride you commute to work in and then shop it around various (wholesale) insurance companies. Once they have received coverage and premium details from each insurance provider they work with, they present it all to you so that you can make a decision about which one to choose. They often then collect a fee from that insurance provider … again for bringing them a customer. A mortgage broker works in a very similar way, except with mortgages instead of insurance.

The wholesale lender is often a bank (though not always) that wants to buy loans originated by someone else in a given geographic area. They don't have loan originators on their staff and they don't speak directly with consumers. They simply take the application the broker obtained from the consumer, underwrite it and ultimately close it. You'll know who the wholesale lender is because, when you sign documents at the closing table, the box marked "Lender" will have the name of the wholesale company on it.

So, there you have it: The three main mortgage lending business models (banks, IMBs and brokers). Now it's up to you to choose which of them you want to work with. Once you do, it's time to get the process started.

Chapter Two

The Application

So, you've decided to buy a home. Or maybe you're refinancing your existing home and want to go into the experience better educated this time so that you're less likely to feel like a mushroom (you know, being left in the dark and fed questionable "info"!). You've done your research and found the best mortgage lending company and loan officer to suit your needs. Now what? It's time to start an application. Decades ago, the mortgage application became standardized. For those in the industry, it's generally referred to as the "app" or the "1003." The 1003 (ten-oh-three) is so named because Fannie Mae (FNMA) issues it as Form 1003. Incidentally, Freddie Mac (FHLMC) has an identical form, but they refer to it as Form 65 (you'll learn more about Fannie Mae and Freddie Mac soon).

The current version of the application has nine different sections and is generally at least seven pages long for each borrower. It can be longer in some circumstances, such as a borrower who is on active duty or a veteran of the military. As you go through page after page of the 1003, there is a good chance you'll feel like you're sitting in a dark room in an uncomfortable chair with a single light shining on you while a plethora of invasive and personal questions are fired at you in rapid succession. There are some people who will tell you that no other transaction (including those related to health care and other financial services) collects more personal private information from you than that needed for a mortgage application. It's possible that one or more of those three-letter government agencies may have more data on you than your mortgage lender, but I'm not positive any of us really know that for sure. The purpose of the inquisition is to start to paint a picture illustrating the likelihood of your repaying your mortgage loan as well as the details of the home that the loan is for. Lending decisions are all about risk. When examining a loan package, questions are asked such as "What is the risk that these people will default on their loan?" and "What is the risk that the subject property will not be sufficient collateral for the loan we are being asked to make?" These are seemingly simple questions, but–to properly analyze that risk–a *ton* of data is needed. If you want to get an idea of what the application looks like, you can do an internet search for "FNMA 1003 download."

Back in my day, an application was generally completed by a loan officer at their desk or the customer's dining-room table by asking each and every question on it and recording the customer's answer. In our current digital world, the vast majority of applications are completed via an online lender portal of some sort. There is a multitude of providers of these online applications and each loan officer you talk with may have one slightly different from the next. However, the information collected by them is the same. It's only the customer experience that will differ from one to the next. Before sitting down to start the application, you would do well to have some information ready. For instance, in section 1, you will be asked (among other things) about a two-year residence history. If you've lived at your current residence for fewer than two years, you'll be asked to provide your previous address and the dates you lived there. If that does not provide a 24-month history, you'll be prompted for a third and so on until that 2-year history is achieved. The same goes for your employment. The application will ask about a minimum of two years' worth of employment history. This will include the company name, address, your position or job title at each employer, your dates of employment and your salary history. If you are self-employed, the level of detail needed will go even deeper. For those lucky folks who are retired, the demands are a little less so long as retirement income can be documented.

You'll also need detailed asset information. In this section 2, you'll be asked about deposit accounts, investment accounts, trusts or any other places you may have some money stashed that can be documented. You'll need institution names, account numbers and balances. The cash you have in the coffee can buried in the backyard or between your mattress and box spring typically cannot be used until it has been in some sort of deposit account long enough to have two consecutive months' worth of account statements showing it being there.

Also found in section 2 are questions on your liabilities. Many of them will be discovered on your credit report once you have given permission for that to be made available. Common debts like car loans, student loans, credit cards and other mortgages should be detailed on the credit report. However, other financial matters like child or spousal support obligations, private notes (loans you may have with private individuals) and non-traditional credit cards may not end up on your credit report but will need to be taken into account when the loan file is examined. Good advice here is to have the details of each liability handy when completing the application. Such details include outstanding balances, payment terms, monthly payments and payments remaining.

Section 3 encompasses details about real estate owned (in industry vernacular, "REO"). If you have property other than the one that's the subject of the loan, your lender will want to know about it. They'll ask about address, value, occupancy (for example, second home, investment property, an empty lot), property taxes, homeowners' insurance and any outstanding loans.

It's not until section 4 (which can usually be found on the fourth page) that you *finally* start to answer questions about the loan you're applying for. Loan amount, loan purpose (purchase, refinance), subject property address, occupancy and existing liens are some of the details that will be asked for here. For those of you looking to refinance your current home, don't forget to have ready for this section details of any second mortgages you may have on the home. It's sometimes easy to forget about that Home Equity Line of Credit (HELOC) when you're completing this section.

Section 5 contains what many mortgage dogs call the "yes/no's." In the current iteration of the 1003, you'll be asked 15 questions with "yes/no" answers to them. They're laborious at best but necessary to complete. They ask questions like have you had a bankruptcy or foreclosure in the past. Do you intend to occupy the property as a primary residence? Do you have outstanding judgements against you or are you in default of federal debt? Again, lots of seemingly invasive questions and, in some cases, a "yes" answer may prompt further questions from your potential lender.

Section 6 is almost an entire page of acknowledgments and agreements. It has 6 subsections and 15 bullet points followed by a signature block to make sure that you attest to having read all of it. Unlike that account agreement you blow past when installing a new app on your phone, it may be worth your time to read through the whole of this section.

Section 7 asks about military service. If you are not serving your country currently (and have not in the past), moving on from this section is as simple as checking the "no" box when asked if you have served. If you have served or are currently serving (I appreciate your service to our country), then all you need to complete the application is to indicate whether you are active, retired or a surviving spouse of a veteran. Don't worry, you'll be asked plenty more later on in the process. For now, it's just a couple of quick questions. But remember: If you answer "yes" to this question, you'll need to have a copy of your DD-214 handy if applying for a loan using your veteran benefits.

Section 8 is demographic information. It asks questions about ethnicity, gender and race. You can choose not to answer these questions: They will have no impact in any way on the outcome of your application. The data is collected as part of the Home Mortgage Disclosure Act (HMDA—pronounced "Hum-Duh!") and submitted to Uncle Sam so that it can provide data to the general public about homeownership rates among different classes. When you see analytics that quantify homeownership among African American, Asian, Hispanic and other ethnicities and races, this is where that data comes from. It helps the government identify where new programs may help benefit homeownership rates within certain demographics that may be underserved. Lastly, this section asks how the application was taken: Face-to-face, over the phone, via the internet or through the mail or fax (yeah, seriously … fax). It's worth noting that, if you decline to answer the demographic questions, federal law requires your loan officer to complete this section based on their visual observation. Why it is that Uncle Sam deems a mortgage lender qualified to make such determinations is beyond me, especially in this melting pot that we all are fortunate to live in.

For those people who can click through a form online and make it sound like Morse code being sent from the Titanic by someone who had *way* too much coffee, completing the application can be done in 15–20 minutes. For others who are sitting at a dining-room table with the application printed out and the blanks being filled in with a pen as the questions are answered, the process may take a bit longer. This is especially so if little Timmy and Fido are having a wrestling match under the table!

The completion of the application is the first step. Next comes the arduous part: The gathering of enough documentation to cripple the aforementioned Titanic. A good loan officer will often warn their clients in advance about the complexity of the documentation that is requested. The good news is that this part is kind of like finishing a concrete slab: The more effort you put into it early on, the easier it will be later in the process. Think about fresh concrete when it's first poured: It is pliable, it can be molded into various shaped forms and it can be finished off with a trowel or float without too much effort. But, if you pour it and then walk away for a bit, it starts to set and the effort required to finish it goes up exponentially. Gathering and submitting the required documentation to your loan officer is very similar: The more work you do up front, the easier it is later in the process.

Compliance

We are now going to digress briefly from the process flow in order to discuss regulatory compliance. This topic can be exceedingly boring. However, having a basic understanding of it will help to illuminate why it is that many of the next steps occur as they do. In the effort to help you navigate the home loan process with a little less stress, it helps to understand the "why" behind aspects that may otherwise seem random or unnecessary. Imagine *not* knowing that the internal combustion engine under the hood of your car ran on gasoline and trying to figure out why it is that you had to stop every so many miles to jam this weird-looking handle into a hole in the side of the car to avoid ending up on the side of the road in Death Valley in August. Understanding why your car needs gas helps to stomach the effort that goes into getting the gas. This perspective is why we are talking about regulatory compliance when almost no one in the world wants to talk about it.

Mortgage banking is considered to be one of the mostly highly regulated industries in the United States and possibly for good reason. For those who lived through the little "issue" in 2008 that led to the Great Recession, you may have heard that it had a lot to do with some unscrupulous lending decisions. We won't go into the details of what caused it because that's a discussion that may better be had over an adult beverage adjacent to six feet of mahogany. However, acknowledging that it occurred gives credence to a plethora of new and updated regulations created post-crisis. The mortgage industry was already highly regulated before that, but regulation increased significantly as a result of some bad decisions in that time frame. *The Dodd-Frank Wall Street Reform and Consumer Protection Act* was one of the outcomes of the Great Recession and (among other things) led to the creation of the Consumer Financial Protection Bureau (CFPB). The CFPB added itself to a number of other federal regulators including the FDIC, the U.S. Department of Housing and Urban Development (HUD), the Federal Housing

Administration (FHA) and the Office of the Comptroller of the Currency (OCC). On a state level, you may also have the Department of Financial Institutions that have regulatory authority and duties. All these regulators lead to what is affectionally called "Alphabet Soup" by compliance officers. Most banking regulations have specific titles (like the Real Estate Settlement Procedures Act—RESPA) and an accompanying letter designation. For instance, CFPB letter classifications for specific regulations include Regulations B, C, D, E, F, G, H, M, N, O, P, V, X, Z, DD and OO. If we include the Federal Reserve Bank regulations, we can add another 19 to that list. The point of all this is that the number of rules and regulations a mortgage lender must follow is huge. Literally tens of thousands of pages of regulations, guidance and requirements have been written. For those suffering from insomnia, I encourage you to study up on the regulations … they may just be what you need for a solid night's sleep.

Disclosures

By now you may be saying, "Okey-dokey, but what does all this have to do with my mortgage application?" It's great that you've asked because here is the answer: Disclosures. Throughout the course of getting a mortgage loan applied for and closed, you'll be presented with pages and pages of disclosures. Many of them are simply for your reading pleasure, but many you'll have to sign before you can move on. Are they necessary? Probably. Are they cumbersome? Absolutely.

The first indication that you're being slapped by the regulation fairy will be shortly after you complete your application. The application itself does not trigger the necessity for you to be given a bunch of disclosures. The trigger is actually just six specific pieces of information: Property address, loan amount, income, estimated value of the property, your name and your social security number. Once those six pieces of information have been collected by your loan officer, they are required by federal regulation to send you certain disclosures within three business days (which *may* include Saturdays) of receipt of them. Chief among these initial disclosures is the Loan Estimate (LE). This provides you with estimates of the costs and fees related to your mortgage loan transaction. These include fees to your lender as well as to third-party service providers such as appraisers, title companies, escrow companies and closing attorneys. Also included will be estimates for pre-paid items such as taxes and insurance. The goal of the LE is to make shopping easier for the consumer. As a prospective borrower, you can take the LE from lender "A" and compare it with the LE from lender "B." This will give you an "apples-to-apples" comparison of costs and fees to help you make your decision regarding with whom you'd like to do business. But a word of wisdom here: The best person to work with is often not the one with the lowest fees or rates. Service and knowledge are paramount in this very complex business. Think about the cheapest car on the lot: It may be easy on your pocketbook, but will it get you to where you need to go quickly, efficiently and without headache? It's often advisable to spend a little extra to ensure that you are getting what you need versus saving money and then not making it to the finish line. Soapbox, dismounted.

I don't want to give you the impression that the LE is representative of the bulk of this first round (commonly referred to as "initial" or "early") of disclosures … because it's not. Far from it.   Each origination company will have slight variations of what is included in the fat stack of documents that will invade your inbox, but in general they will look largely the same. Expect to be asked to look through anywhere from 15–20 different documents, most of which are multiple pages. Among what seems like a ream of paper worth of "stuff," you'll most likely find the following: A copy of your loan application, a list of local homeownership counseling providers, the borrower's certification and authorization (more on this shortly), an affiliated business arrangement disclosure statement, a privacy policy, a copy of the Fair Credit Reporting Act, your home loan toolkit and an Internal Revenue Service (IRS) transcript request. There will be more than what has been listed here and a few that are listed may be absent. Why are you having to deal with all of these? Compliance with federal regulations, that's why. There are a couple I'd like to call attention to because of the critical timing that may be involved with them.

1. The Borrower's Certification and Authorization: This relatively simple document requires your signature and the sooner you can do that, the better. The "cause why" is because it allows your loan officer to work on your behalf to acquire necessary items, thereby lessening the

burden on you to obtain information and/or documents. By signing the document, you *certify* that you give *authorization* for your lender to obtain personal data specific to you from third parties. An example would be a payoff for a current liability, such as the existing mortgage you're looking to refinance or a car loan you want to pay off using the equity in your home. If you are refinancing your home, your lender will need to determine exactly how much you owe on your current mortgage so that, when it is paid off during the home loan refinance, they will pay off the correct amount (down to the penny). If you're paying off additional debt, the document will allow your lender to acquire details on that as well. Without the ability to do this, things can get dicey: Imagine you want to pay off a car loan but you don't have an accurate payoff statement and too little is sent to the creditor. The clear title you can't wait to get in the mail may never come.

2. The IRS Transcript Request: This document is IRS form 4506-C and is commonly referred to as such in the industry. Once it is signed by you, it allows your lender to obtain a copy of your tax returns (or other tax-related documents) from the IRS. Why would they need this when you can and probably will, provide copies from your own files? Well, believe it or not, there are some not-so-honest consumers out there who may alter their tax returns to reflect more income than actually reported. Similarly, there have been some lenders who would alter your

tax return for you so that it reflects an income higher than it should be in order for you to qualify for a larger loan than would be possible using your "real" income. Getting a copy of the tax return transcripts directly from the IRS allows the lender and/or investor to verify that the income declared in the loan file matches what Uncle Sam was told. It keeps everyone honest.

Receiving, reviewing and completing these disclosures is a time-sensitive exercise. There are some aspects of building the loan file that cannot happen until you have completed these steps. For instance, that Borrower's Certification and Authorization is needed before starting to collect the data necessary to accurately represent the loan transaction. There are also third-party services that have to be ordered on your behalf, such as an appraisal of the home, whereby expenses are incurred. If an order is put in before you review the LE and give your intent to proceed, then—legally—you are not required to pay that expense because you have not yet authorized it. And that authorization cannot be given by you until after you have reviewed the LE and given your consent. See ... the government *is* here to help—It just does so in an exceptionally complex way!

Okay, enough on disclosures: You'll become intimately familiar with these whether you like it or not—because of regulatory compliance. But, for now, let's talk instead about documenting your life.

Regard this simple concept: If you're applying for a loan, you're going to need to show you have a way to repay that loan. If Craig asks his mom to lend him $200 the day after he got fired from his job for stealing boxes (on his day off no less), mom is probably going to reply with "I'm not comfortable lending you money without a job." Mom is wise … don't mess with mom. Applying for a mortgage loan is no different. Your lender will need to document your *qualifying* income in order to accurately represent your ability to repay the loan. Note the emphasis on "qualifying" in the preceding sentence. This is because not all income can be used to determine your ability to repay the loan. In order to simplify this concept as much as possible, let's establish that "qualifying income" is generally income that is reported to the IRS. That can complicate things for self-employed individuals or "gig workers" who may get paid under the table. If you are self-employed, you may make good money but your skilled Certified Public Accountant (CPA) is good at utilizing legal tax codes to effectively reduce your taxable income. There is nothing nefarious about this: It's simply the way most business owners operate because it reduces the amount of taxes they need to pay. The drawback is that, when applying for a traditional mortgage loan, your lender must qualify you based on the income reported to the IRS. So, in real life you may make very good money but, in the eyes of Uncle Sam, you may make very little— thereby reducing the size of the loan you can qualify for. This scenario can be particularly unpleasant for a lender when their customer is an affluent individual who is under the impression they can afford darn near anything but who also has a very good CPA who drastically reduces their taxable income. If you fall into this category, talk to your lender and ask about unique programs that are designed for business owners and offered by some investors. You may have some options to work with.

For the average person who gets paid as a W2 employee (not self-employed and gets paid hourly or on a salary), the process is much simpler. Generally, you'll be asked for a couple of years' worth of tax returns and/or W2s and a recent paystub or two. Each investor may have a slightly different requirement for documenting the "W2 income" so what you are asked for may vary slightly, but the two years of taxes and two most recent paystubs are pretty common.

As the complexity of your income(s) increases, so does the complexity of the documentation necessary to prove it. We touched on self-employed business owners, who are near the top of the complexity spectrum. Somewhere below that comes retired individuals, those with income from trusts, newly employed people, seasonal workers, contract employees, those with bonus' or overtime and folks with a work or student visa. I'd go into detail on each scenario, but the guidelines that apply to each example are pages and pages long and are only really needed by your loan officer and the underwriter who will render the decision on your loan (hopefully to approve it).

Once your total annual income is determined, the size of the loan you qualify for will be largely influenced by the total proposed debt load (right about now, I'd be asking "What the heck is total proposed debt load?"). It's not a stretch to imagine that, if someone makes $65,000 per year and their mortgage payment for their new house is $5,000 per month, there is not much left for other necessities like food, clothes, electricity and baseball cards for the spokes of their bicycle. There is a general rule (and, remember, rules are made to be broken) that a mortgage lender is looking to qualify you based on your total monthly debt obligations not exceeding 43% of your total gross income. The 43% benchmark is not set in stone. In some cases, it can be as high as 50% and in others it may be as low as 36%. It depends on the investor and the loan product. Loan products guaranteed or insured by the Federal Housing Administration (FHA) or the U.S. Department of Veterans Affairs (VA) often allow that debt ratio to be higher than 43%. Some jumbo investors (a jumbo loan is a loan amount higher than the conforming loan limit—see the Glossary for details) limit the total debt ratio to 36%. Not all expenses you'd expect are factored into the debt ratio. For instance, things like utilities, cell phone bills and auto insurance are not included in that calculation. You can count on the obligations listed on your credit report to be factored into the calculation and you'll be asked about any additional undisclosed debt obligations you may have (like the loan from Uncle Rico to buy the sweet corduroy tuxedo). And, of

course, the proposed mortgage payment of the loan
you are applying for is included in the debt ratio.

Chapter Three

Assets

I think my wife has great assets, but those aren't the kind we are talking about here! When your loan officer asks for your assets, they are looking for documentation to prove that you have some money—sort of like income has to be of the "qualified" type, assets do as well. Cash in the gun safe or buried in the backyard won't be looked upon as "qualified assets." I've been asked a few times why one needs to provide assets when applying for a loan. After all, if you had assets, you may not need a loan, right? Well, there are costs involved in obtaining a mortgage loan. Closing costs, fees to the lender and/or third-party vendors (appraisers, inspectors, title companies, etc.) all must be paid. Sometimes they can be paid using part of the loan you're applying for, but often that is not the case. If you are buying a home, your down payment must come from qualified assets. For some types of loans, you may be required to have a few months' worth of mortgage payments on hand in the event of a loss of income. These are called "reserves" and have to be documented from … wait for it … qualified assets.

What the heck defines "qualified assets"? Greenbacks that can be "sourced and seasoned" is the answer to that question. Sourced: Can be verified via an account statement from some institution (think a savings account statement). Seasoned: Have been in the documented account for at least two months. The "sourced" part is what eliminates the ability to use the $20 from grandma on your birthday because it resides in a greeting card, not a deposit account. The same reasoning applies to mattress money, the cash buried in the yard, piggy banks and so on. The "seasoned" part is because, if you have had it in a verified account for at least two months, the likelihood that those funds came from a newly acquired loan that is not documented on your credit report goes down significantly. Imagine you are going to buy a home and your Uncle Rico is rich because back in '82 he went pro after proving he could throw a football over the mountains. He hooks you up with a loan of $20,000 to use as your down payment at the friends and family rate of 10% interest compounded monthly until you pay it back. That $20k shows up on your savings account five weeks ago. When your loan officer gets a copy of that savings account statement, they are going to ask about the source of it. If Uncle Rico was generous and gave it to you instead of lending it to you, then you only have to get a "gift letter" from him saying it's a gift and there is no need for you to repay it. If he is less generous and it's a loan to be repaid at 10% interest, then your loan officer will have to add that to your list of monthly obligations, thereby reducing the total amount you can qualify for.

The other reason for sourcing and seasoning funds is a little more dramatic. There was a time when criminal enterprises would launder money through mortgage transactions. Imagine someone named Tony is the drug kingpin of Florida. You are making cash hand over fist and your depository banker raises his rates on you to clean the money, prompting you to find other ways to do it that take less off your overhead. If you used that cash to buy a house with a 50% down payment, then sold the house a couple of years later, your dirty money is now clean. In that scenario, the cash for the down payment was probably deposited into a bank account shortly before the transaction took place, or maybe it was used to buy a cashier's check to take to closing. Either way, it wasn't sourced or seasoned and a federally backed mortgage loan was just used to launder money with criminal intent. The same logic applies to terrorists trying to finance homes using ill-gotten gains.

Qualified assets can take many forms. The simplest and most common are deposit accounts like checking or savings accounts. But you're able to use other accounts as well: Investment accounts, retirement accounts, life insurance policies with cash value and even stock accounts. Some of these have special stipulations to them that may decrease their face value, but they are none-the-less "qualified." Be prepared to hand over two of the most recent statements for whatever account you plan to use to establish assets. Also, you should be warned that you will be asked to document "large deposits" into your account. A large deposit is defined as any deposit that exceeds 50% of your total monthly qualifying income. The reasoning behind this is similar to the Uncle Rico example: If a large sum of money shows up in your account, the lender will want to know if it came from a new debt that you will be obligated to. A unique example of a large deposit happened when Rodney the rancher submitted his bank statements while applying for a home loan. On that statement was a deposit of $12,000 the previous month and, since this was in excess of his qualifying monthly income, he was asked to document its source. He later submitted a bill of sale for a prize-winning pig he had sold for $12,000 to help finance the purchase of his new home (true story). It was a legitimate deposit that wasn't the result of new debt, so all was well (probably except for the pig).

Loan products

If you have provided all the requested documentation, the chances are you're exhausted; maybe a little frustrated; certainly ready to get the ball rolling. The good news is that it's time to start making some decisions about how to proceed. There's a multitude of loan products available to consumers so the best solution can be found. Your loan officer will examine all the information you have provided and then present you with some options to choose from. The number of options always varies based on the unique circumstances of each applicant as well as the products available to each lender. We'll cover the most common here.

The fixed-rate mortgage

The fixed-rate mortgage is the most common product found in the United States. It's pretty simple and somewhat self-explanatory. The interest rate on your Note (The "IOU" where you promise to repay the loan) is fixed for the life of the loan. Regardless of what happens in the markets, your rate will not rise or fall once it is locked. A quick note on a rate lock: Mortgage interest rates fluctuate. If markets are volatile, they may go up or down (or both) multiple times in one day. More likely, you'll see them change from day to day. Until your rate is locked in, it's subject to change. If your loan officer quotes you a rate at 9:00 a.m. and you don't respond instructing them to lock it in until later that afternoon, it's possible that rate will no longer be available depending on market volatility at that time. If you are presented with a rate you find acceptable, you'd be well advised to lock it in swiftly. You can "play the game" and hope the rate improves by waiting it out but, in my experience, more than 50% of the time that game is played by a consumer, they lose. The rate you lock in will determine the principal and interest portion of your monthly payment. On a fixed-rate product, that will not change for the life of the loan. However, keep in mind that your monthly payment is comprised of four parts: principal, interest, taxes and insurance. These are commonly referred to as "PITI." On a fixed-rate mortgage, the principal and interest (P&I) portions are predictable. Early in the life of the loan, a large percentage of your monthly payment will be allocated to interest while a smaller portion goes to the reduction of principal. Each month you make a payment, a little less goes to interest and a little more goes to principal. Regardless of the allocation to each, the sum of those two parts (P&I) will always be the same (plus or minus a cent or so due to rounding). The taxes and insurance part (T&I) changes, usually from year to year. "Taxes" refers to your property taxes. Those are typically dictated by the county and sometimes the city. "Insurance" is your homeowners insurance, commonly referred to as "hazard insurance." As the value of your property changes year over year (hopefully goes UP!!!), your taxes will often go up as well. Insurance can do the same thing. As the cost to insure a home goes up for the insurance companies, they pass that cost on to you as the homeowner. It is because of these changes to taxes and insurance that even your "fixed rate-mortgage" payment will change from time to time. Like most homeowners, you will get an annual escrow account disclosure that gives you a bunch of information about the account your loan servicer uses to house and distribute your loan payments. This has a lot of data, but most notably it will usually be your first clue that your monthly mortgage payment will be changing. Fret not, for there is a silver lining: It's not fun to pay more money each month, but, if your payment goes up, you can take solace in the knowledge that it's probably due to the value of your home going up too.

Jumbo versus conforming

Images of a conformist generally conjure up some sort of Dudley Do-Right with perfectly parted hair, a smart shirt neatly pressed, trousers and a corporate "yes man" attitude. When talking mortgages with your friends at happy hour, "conforming" has nothing to do with fitting a square peg into a perfectly machined square hole: It has to do with loan amount. A conforming loan has a loan amount that is not in excess of the defined amount set forth by the Federal Housing Finance Agency (FHFA). The FHFA, among other things, is the regulating body of FNMA, FHLMC and the Federal Home Loan Banks. Part of its duties is to establish the "conforming loan limit." That limit defines the size of the loans to be purchased by FNMA and FHLMC and it is reassessed annually with the new limit being effective on January 1 of each calendar year. If you do an internet search for "conforming loan limit," it will be revealed to you for the current year as well as all previous years dating back to the early 1980s when it was $93,750.

When you exceed the conforming loan limit by even one cent, you've entered jumbo loan territory. A "jumbo loan" is the term assigned to any loan in excess of the conforming loan limit. These loans are ineligible for delivery to Fannie Mae or Freddie Mac. They are usually purchased by private investors (more on this to be found in the "Agency versus private" chapter) and, as such, have different qualification guidelines compared with their conforming counterparts.

The adjustable-rate mortgage

Homes are expensive. Some may say they cost an arm and a leg. If you subscribe to that nomenclature, then maybe you'll want to get a mortgage loan product that is in line with it. The adjustable-rate mortgage (ARM) came into popularity during the early 1980s when mortgage rates approached 20%. Interest rates on ARMs are generally lower than those associated with the fixed-rate products when they are locked in. As the name implies, they also adjust with the changes in the market. The lower rate is attractive to the homeowner (for obvious reasons) and the adjustability is attractive to the investor. Why would the investor like the adjustability? It keeps their investment viable in a changing environment. If the investor holds a Note on a fixed-rate mortgage at 5% and over the years the rates go up to 7%, then that investor has a fair bit of money tied up at a rate of return (5%) that is far lower than that in the current market (7%): Hence, their fondness for adjustable-rate products.

ARM interest rates adjust at a predetermined interval based on a formula identified by the product. That formula consists of a static component called the "margin" and a variable called the "index." The margin is identified by the loan product description that your loan officer will have available. It might be something like 2.75% or thereabouts. The index comes into play at the time of each rate adjustment and is also identified by that same loan product description. You'll find many indices that can be used for ARM products, but most products use one of just two or three of the most common ones. The Secured Overnight Financing Rate (SOFR) index recently replaced the London Interbank Offered Rate (LIBOR) as the most commonly used index for these products.

Some ARMs adjust as frequently as once a month (though very rare) and others are fixed for an introductory period and then adjust annually thereafter. The latter are the most common and are called "hybrid ARMs." No, this has nothing to do with a mortgage product powered by fossil *and* renewable energy: Rather, it is because they are fixed for an introductory period and then automatically adjust annually afterward. The length of the introductory fixed period changes from product to product. However, you'll most commonly see them "fixed" for five, seven, or ten years. These are referred to as 5/1, 7/1 and 10/1 ARMS (pronounced "five-one ARM", etc.). The numbers say it all: A 5/1 ARM is fixed for the first five years and then adjusts each year thereafter. The same logic applies to the 7/1 and 10/1 hybrid ARMS as well.

To better understand the product, let's use the 10/1 ARM as an example. Once your loan closes, the Note rate you locked in will be used to calculate the principal and interest portions of your monthly payment for the first 120 months (10 years). After that initial "fixed" period has passed, your 10/1 ARM will begin to adjust annually (starting at month 121) based on the margin assigned to the product and the index it is keyed from. If we use 2.75% as the pre-determined (and unchanging) margin, we then add to it the index at the time of adjustment. If that index is 1.71% (random numbers used for this example), then your new Note rate at month 121 will be 4.46%. Please keep in mind that these numbers are pulled out of thin air and in no way represent the actual rate you may have. The numbers change daily, but the formula remains the same.

But you forward-thinking mathletes out there may be asking, "What if the market has gone WAY up during those first 120 months? Will my new rate be way higher, making for a much higher monthly payment?" The short answer is: "Yes, it's possible." But there is a silver lining to that ominous cloud too and this is called "caps." One of the defining characteristics of an ARM product is that each one comes with a set of "caps" that limit the extent at which the rate can change at any one adjustment as well as over the life of the loan. To your 10/1 ARM example, we are going to assign 5/2/5 caps (which are pretty common and very realistic outside our example). To understand what this means, we take each number in sequence, starting with the first "5." At the time of the first adjustment (month 121), the most the rate can possibly adjust to is 5%. So, in an extreme case, if the introductory/fixed rate were 4% for the first 120 months, it could increase to as much as 9% at the first adjustment if the market had moved that much. That's a worst-case example. That first cap is conveniently called the "initial adjustment cap." The second number in this case is 2. What this tells us is that, once your first adjustment has occurred, each subsequent adjustment can be no more than 2%, making future market rate adjustments a bit easier to stomach when the market rate continues to go up. The final number is the max adjustment over the life of the loan. In this case, your Note rate would never go up more than 5% over the life of the loan (indicated by the second "5" in 5/2/5). If that first adjustment happens to reach the extreme of 5%, then your Note rate will never go above 9% in our example—no matter how much higher the market goes. And, since the life cap is also 5%, that would mean your first adjustment would also be the last you'd ever see unless the market went down. In a less extreme example, maybe your first adjustment is only 1% making the new Note rate 5% at month 121. The next year, it may go up again if the market dictates, but it can't go up any more than 2% at any one adjustment for the rest of the term of the loan. These caps work in your favor to limit the extent of the adjustments for as long as you have the adjustable-rate mortgage.

Chapter Four

Federal Housing Administration/Veterans Affairs

"We're with the government and we're here to help!" Say that to someone and you may get an eye roll. However, when it comes to mortgage loan programs, the FHA and VA products *are* government-sponsored programs and they *do* help. Is one or the other right for you? Let's find out.

The FHA is part of the U.S. Department of Housing and Urban Development. How does that effect you? It absolutely does not. But it sets the tone for a government-oriented loan program that we will be highlighting. The FHA provides mortgage insurance for loans that are created by FHA-approved lending institutions. The benefits of the FHA loan programs are often realized by soon-to-be homeowners who may not necessarily qualify for the more well-known conventional loan programs associated with Fannie Mae or Freddie Mac. The requirements to qualify for an FHA loan are less stringent than the aforementioned conventional products. They allow for lower credit scores, higher debt ratios and low down payments (as low as 3.5%). They are offered on most property types such as manufactured homes, condominiums and, of course, single-family residences. They have occupancy restrictions, meaning that you must occupy the home as your primary residence. There is an exception made for multi-unit dwellings like a duplex where you occupy one unit as your primary residence and the other can be rented out.

With all these wonderful traits, there are a couple of differences from conventional loans that should be noted. For example, the mortgage insurance on an FHA loan program is for the life of the loan. With conventional programs, mortgage insurance can often be removed once a certain loan-to-value is achieved. Also, the qualification requirements may be a bit different from lender to lender. Just because the FHA allows for a credit score down to 500 does not mean your lender is comfortable with that. They may have an overlay that requires a higher credit score.

All that said, it can be a great option for someone with a checkered credit history, not a lot of money for a down payment, or who does not make a lot of money. They are generally popular with first-time homebuyers looking to start building wealth with the purchase of their first home, which may not necessarily be their forever home.

The VA offers a partial guarantee on mortgage loans for qualified individuals. This guarantee is in lieu of the mortgage insurance found on other mortgage loans with loan-to-values above 80%. The VA also offers this with a no down payment requirement, which is awesome. Similar to an FHA loan, the credit score requirements are typically lower while the debt ratio maximums are higher and also designed for owner-occupied properties.

Sounds wonderful right? Well, not everyone gets to take advantage of these amazing programs. VA loan programs are only available to qualified active duty, reservists or honorably discharged veterans of our U.S. military. To qualify, one must have served in the military for at least 181 consecutive days during peacetime or at least 90 days if any of those were during wartime. If an applicant has served fewer than those stipulated days or were other than honorably discharged, the eligibility goes away. In some cases, surviving spouses of a service member who passed away while serving or from a service-related disability, became a prisoner of war, or became missing in action, may also qualify. The other notable benefit is that the lender is limited on the fees they can charge on a VA loan. This benefit was huge in the days before the Great Recession of 2008 when lenders were price-gouging consumers like a street vendor peddling cheap imported goods. It's less of a benefit in current times because the fees charged on mortgage loans are much more reasonable due to regulation. If you're on active duty or a veteran, it would be wise to explore this option when purchasing or refinancing a home.

U.S. Department of Agriculture

While we are on the topic of government-sponsored programs that allow a zero-down payment option, let's talk about the U.S. Department of Agriculture. No, we're not asking you to finance a chicken coop with no down payment. I'm referring to the U.S. Department of Agriculture (USDA) Rural

Development Guaranteed Housing Loan Program. A mouthful? You can bet the farm it is! Luckily, it's commonly referred to as "RD" for Rural Development. It's a pretty cool program that kills two birds with one frozen cow pie. The first is a zero-down option for folks who aren't laden with excess cash and may not be able to afford a traditional mortgage. Second, it helps finance rural properties that are not looked upon with a lustful eye by the traditional lending products out there. Some of the most common options for home financing are not fond of rural properties or larger acreages. This is because it's hard to find other properties with similar characteristics to help determine the value (more on that when we discuss appraisals).

RD loans are similar to VA loans in that they have a guarantee on them by Uncle Sam in the event of a default. Because of this, rates on them are generally a bit lower than conventional loans and there are options for zero-down payments. Unlike the VA, they do have mortgage insurance associated with them (they are a little more like the FHA in that regard). There are income limits for qualification, meaning that, if you make too much money, you aren't eligible. There are also limits on debt ratios, citizenship and credit history. But don't get your hopes up for an RD loan option on a home in a metropolitan area. As the name "Rural Development" implies, these loan options are geared more toward "Green Acres" versus the green beltways of urban living. And not all lenders are approved with USDA to make RD loans. So, if ya'll think this is your ticket to turn that pavement princess into a legit farm truck, check to make sure that your loan originator is approved to get you an RD loan. If not, you may need to call Billy-Bob Home Lending [Drops mic and spits with a "clang" into the spittoon!]

Chapter Five

Agency versus private

When you hear "agency," you may think "Central Intelligence." When "private" comes up, your mind may wander to a diary where your deepest darkest secrets are "safely" recorded, waiting for someone's little brother to pick the lock and read. Fortunately, neither of those are true because they apply to mortgage lending. Here, they have to do with who buys and/or guarantees the mortgage loan you just signed your life away on for the privilege of making payments over the next 30 years. If you're standing at the water cooler in a mortgage lending office and someone refers to the "agencies," they are generally referring to Freddie Mac or Fannie Mae. The more formal title for each of them is "government-sponsored enterprise" (GSE). They aren't the only GSEs that exist, but they are the most popular and common.

The question of whether an agency or a private investor will be purchasing your loan may seem innocuous. However, it can have a pretty profound impact on the origination of your loan and it's worth noting. "Why?" you may ask. Simply put, it determines how complicated the process may be. An agency loan is by far the most common type of loan out there. They are crafted and underwritten based on a set of guidelines set forth by either Fannie Mae or Freddie Mac. Fannie and Freddie have extensive guidelines published that dictate how a lender must create a loan file in order for it to qualify to be purchased by either of the agencies. That may seem quite dictatorial in nature considering every homeowner has a very different scenario. However, it also provides a great deal of consistency in the origination of the loan. It can make for a great customer service experience because the loan officer and underwriter know exactly what they need to do in order to manufacture a good loan file. That makes surprises along the way much less frequent and provides a quality loan officer with the ability to accurately convey what the borrower can expect early in the process.

Private investors are a different story. While many of them follow many of the same guidelines that Fannie and Freddie publish, the fact is that, when it's *their* money, they get to add to those guidelines as they see fit. To put this in perspective, recall a derivation of the Golden Rule: "He/she who has the gold makes the rules." Let's say you won the lottery and have a ton of available cash at your fingertips. And with that cash you decide to go into business as a lender for others seeking to borrow money. Since it's your money, you get to dictate the terms of the loan. Maybe you will only lend to someone who has a *really* high credit score. Maybe you only accept gold bullion as collateral. Or perhaps your lending standards are somewhat relaxed, but in return you're going to charge 37.375% interest. However (un)reasonable your terms are, the fact of the matter is that you have the money and the customer wants to borrow it, so they must adhere to whatever terms you dictate. Private mortgage investors can do the same. It's not that they have unreasonable standards: They just choose to have terms that are often different and possibly more restrictive than the agencies. Their guidelines are also published. However, they may look at things differently from the more commonly known and understood agencies. Who are these private investors? They are generally large banks and/or financial institutions that we have all heard of. Basically, any institution or investor that is not in some way affiliated with a government program could be considered a private investor. Fannie, Freddie, the Federal Home Loan Bank and guarantors or insurers like the FHA, VA and USDA do not fall in to the "private" category. Practically speaking, all others would.

If you are applying for a mortgage loan from your loan officer that is not an agency loan, there is a higher likelihood that some additional items may be asked for that weren't known or understood on day one of the loan application process. Private lender underwriters have the latitude to request additional documentation on a more frequent and/or unpredictable manner than agency programs. This isn't all bad though. Private investors will often do things that Fannie and Freddie won't. Jumbo loans are a good example. "Alternative documentation" is another. Maybe, instead of using paystubs to determine income, a private investor might accept bank statements that show income on them. Often, private investors can make loans that wouldn't stand a snowball's chance in an eternally hot place with the agencies.

Fannie Mae and Freddie Mac

Hinted at in the "Agency vs. private" section, Fannie Mae (commonly referred to by "her" first name, Fannie) and Freddie Mac (similarly, "he" is known as Freddie) are the two most common government-sponsored enterprises (GSEs). In the long run, this knowledge may not affect you one iota. However, where I think it has value is in understanding what these two entities do, because in recent history they have played spectacularly huge roles in domestic economic policy. And their huge impact on the entirety of the American economy all boils down to the payment you make every month on your mortgage. That's right, YOU and those like you can have an impact on the domestic economy … in a small way.

Fannie and Freddie are guarantors of loans. Sure, they do other things too like buy loans, set guidelines on which loan decisions are based and heavily influence the interest rate that the average American consumer pays when getting a loan. But it's the guarantee they offer that sets the tone for mortgage lending in our great country. When a conforming loan is made, it's typically sold after being closed. It may be sold to Fannie, Freddie or an "aggregator." An aggregator is a mortgage company that buys individual loans from all the smaller lenders all over the country and then puts all these individual loans into a bag of loans with similar characteristics. They then sell this bag of loans to investors. What makes a bag of loans attractive to an investor is (among other things) the guarantee that Fannie and/or Freddie offer on them. The guarantee says that, even if the homeowner does not make their mortgage payment, the investor will still receive their payment of both principal and interest (P&I). There are several nuances to this, involving complicated things like "remittance types" that are discussions for that same six feet of mahogany and beverage that have been mentioned before. For simplicity's sake, we'll just assume that Fannie and Freddie make sure that the investor is paid their P&I regardless of how diligent the person is about making their mortgage payment(s).

So that's cool: the investor gets paid no matter how the underlying security performs. But what about when a catastrophic economic downturn happens? Something like what happened around 2008? You had all those people not making their payments on their mortgages for one reason or another. Fannie and Freddie are paying out to investors like it's Christmas morning to the tune of *billions* of dollars. Eventually the 'ole checkbook will run a little thin. Despite the implied nature of GSEs, they didn't (at that time) have Uncle Sam's checkbook. That is when the government stepped in and said, "We're here to help." Their method of helping is to take Fannie and Freddie into conservatorship, thereby effectively giving them the key to the federal reserve. It's a lot easier to keep investors happy when you have Fort Knox in the back yard. But one of the drawbacks is that, when you are given all the cash you need to pay the bills, you get your checkbook taken away. And, as of now, Fannie and Freddie are still living in conservatorship, with only a portion of their earnings not going to the Treasury. That's the 25-cent version of the story of how the government saved the two largest guarantors of the trillion-dollar mortgage-backed security market.

Now the story of how the same government used the same mortgage guarantors to keep the economy moving forward during the largest economic shutdown in the history of planet Earth (and I think Mars too). You may remember a little hiccup in all our daily lives round about March of 2020. Production of face masks and hand sanitizer went up when virtually every other segment of the economy stopped. Some exceptions to this were home shopping services, streaming video … and mortgages. If no one is spending money because they are "social distancing" from home, then it's tough to keep an economy moving forward. Solution? Throw as much money at the economy as you can, as quickly as you can. And what is the single largest purchase most people make? A home. It's easy to get half a million dollars in the hands of consumers if you help them buy houses instead of steak dinners out on date nights. So, the Federal Reserve gave Fannie and Freddie what was almost an open checkbook to buy mortgages. They bought mortgages like Mr. Goldfinger bought gold bullion while James Bond was entertaining his assistant. And they were buying at a premium. It would have been like them buying your beige 1996 Toyota Corolla for $104,000. It injected a ton of cash into the economy. Of course, the aftermath of it all was teaching everyone the consequences of printing money quicker than a second-grader can turn out stick figures with a dull red crayon.

Unfortunately, this astronomically high-level view of Fannie Mae and Freddie Mac doesn't do them justice. They are an integral part of the mortgage industry and equally important in the domestic economy. I'll leave this topic with a funny story: As a young elementary school-aged boy with two parents who were active in the mortgage industry conference circuit, I was inundated with pens, pencils, note pads and various other swag that they brought home with them. By the time I was in fifth grade, I had been asked dozens of times why my grandmother's name was on all my pencils. After all, what else would a child deduce from "Fannie Mae" being embossed on every piece of stationery I had?

Chapter Six

Interest rates

For many in the market for a home loan, the topic of interest rate is the "brass tacks" of the discussion. The average loan officer will probably tell you that, when taking the first call from a consumer inquiring about a mortgage loan, nine out of ten times they will be asked "What's your rate?" If/when you ask this question, remember that there are many factors that enter into determining the rate on a given mortgage loan. And under almost zero circumstances can that rate be accurately determined on the first call to a loan officer. There are simply too many factors involved. Any rate given out before sufficient documentation and information have been obtained is no more than a shot in the dark. You may get close, but the chances of it being a bullseye are slim to none. The interest rate (or Note Rate) is essentially the cost of borrowing money. If you borrow $100,000, you end up repaying significantly more than the $100,000 principal balance of the loan. That is because of interest. In general, interest is calculated annually, based on the loan's principal balance and paid monthly (as part of your monthly mortgage payment). As you pay down your loan, the amount of your monthly payment attributed to interest also decreases. A good visual illustration of this is the amortization schedule you are given at the closing table. This details how much of your monthly payment goes toward P&I (as well as taxes and insurance if appropriate). The lower your interest rate, the lower the total cost of borrowing the money.

Annual Percentage Rate

Most people focus on the interest rate when shopping for a mortgage and understandably so. After all, whoever has the lowest interest rate on their mortgage gets the bragging rights over a pint at the pub. The interest rate is the cost of borrowing the money, *before* any additional fees and/or costs are factored in. Think of it as the rate your lender uses when they calculate the interest portion of your monthly mortgage payment. The Annual Percentage Rate (APR) shows the total cost of borrowing, including interest rate *and* fees. It's the calculation on an annual basis of the total interest paid on the loan amount plus any additional charges and it represents a truer annual cost of the loan if you were to take the loan to term (meaning you don't pay it off early). Things like origination and discount fees (commonly referred to as "Points"), as well as other charges like underwriting or processing fees, are often required on a mortgage loan and must be accounted for when comparing one lender's offer with another's. When shopping one lender against another, the APR is a better "apples-to-apples" comparison versus interest rate alone.

Chapter Seven

Appraisals

"**D**on't try to lowball me, I know what I've got!" If you're Craigslist connoisseur, you're all too familiar with the concept that the value assigned to something by the seller is not often congruent with that of the buyer. That beige 1996 Corolla that has always been garaged, oil changed every 3,000 miles and waxed quarterly may not be worth the premium the seller thinks it is. Houses are the same. A quality real estate agent can often identify the market price of a home based on their experience. However, it is the value placed on it by a licensed real estate appraiser that ultimately determines how your purchase or refinance transaction will go. An appraisal is a valuation of a property that is performed by a licensed appraiser and serves a number of purposes beyond determining what it is worth. The appraised value is a key component in determining how much you can borrow. Sure, your income and expenses play a very large role in that as well. However, even if you make all the money in the world, a lender will only lend you a percentage of the value of the home. This ratio between loan amount and home value is called the "loan to value" ratio (LTV for short). Lending institutions want to make sure that there is some equity in the property in the event that they have to foreclose on the home (with the notable exception of VA and RD loans). To ensure this, they will only lend up to a percentage of the value of the home. That maximum percentage is different depending on loan programs, lenders and other factors like whether you will occupy the home as your primary residence, as a second home, or if it will be used as a rental. For simplicity's sake, let's say that your lender will only loan you money up to 90% of the value of the home. That's great … but how is the value determined? That's where an appraiser swoops in and saves the day. Appraisers go through years of training before they become licensed to place a value on a piece of real estate. They are professionals, folks, so don't try this on your own home. If Alice Appraiser determines that your home is worth $500,000 and your lender will lend you up to 90% of the value, then—assuming all goes well—you can borrow up to $450,000 using your home as collateral. That seems like a pretty simple idea. However, the appraisal itself is quite complex, often being 40–50 pages in length containing an inordinate amount of data that would make Commander Data fry a pathway in his neural network. Don't worry: You'll get to see it for yourself. Federal law mandates that a consumer be given a copy of the appraisal at least three business days before the close of their loan. Generally, you'll get a copy well in advance of closing—Because: Regulatory compliance.

The amount of research and data that goes into determining the value of a home goes way beyond the scope of this book. In fact, an entire book could be written on appraisals alone. And rest assured that, when a lender is considering a loan of $450,000, they look at every line on every page of that appraisal. They want to make sure that the collateral you are pledging is acceptable in every way. No one wants to lend six-digits' worth of greenbacks based on a three-bedroom two-bath made of mud and clay nestled in the wastelands of some mosquito-infested swamp that even Master Yoda wouldn't consider: "Pile of sticks they don't want."

When you get a copy of your appraisal, you'll probably learn more about your home than you possibly imagined. Detailed in the plethora of pages will be square footage calculations, a legal description, year built and condition of everything from the landscaping to the attic. You'll also find pictures of the interior and exterior of the home, home value trends in the neighborhood, any improvements made, details of the sales contract (if you're purchasing it), site information and—of course—sales comparisons. "Comps" is the common term to refer to *comp*arable houses nearby that have recently sold and are used to help determine the value of your home (referred to as the "subject property"). If we refer back to the 1996 Corolla you're looking to put in the garage, a good way to determine the value is to look at other 1996 Corollas that were recently sold to see what they went for. You'd want to look for cars that were similar in mileage, condition and options and were cared for in the same manner. If you can find three to five of those that fit the bill, then they can provide a benchmark to determine what your new ride might be worth. This is called a "sales comparison" approach and is the same way an appraiser will determine the value of your new primary residence.

Just like anything else, some appraisals are done better than others. It behooves you to review yours and look for any glaring mistakes. Things like square footage, bedroom/bathroom count, size of garage or lot size inaccuracies can have an adverse impact on the true value of the home. If you are refinancing, no one (including the appraiser) knows your home better than you. Take a moment to look through the appraisal after it's given to you to make sure it all looks correct. I would caution anyone against trying to determine the value themselves. However, identifying incorrect attributes in the home can help in creating the most accurate appraisal possible.

The type of construction can have a significant impact on value and lendability as well. If we play the age-old game of word association whereby someone says a word and you reply with the first thing that comes to mind, "Home" probably elicits a response similar to "3-bedroom, 2-bath, double car garage with a white picket fence and 2.3 kids playing with 1.5 dogs on the front lawn". That is great and there are certainly plenty of those in the world. However, there are other options for those looking to get in on the American dream of homeownership. Other construction methods and styles are plentiful. Geodesic homes, log homes, modular and manufactured homes are all examples of real-world alternatives to the traditional stick-built homes that Beaver Cleaver grew up in. Modular homes are becoming more and more popular due to the efficiency with which they can be constructed as well as the consistency of their manufacturing, given that this is generally in a climate-controlled warehouse in an assembly-line style of construction. Manufactured homes are good options for first-time home buyers when the cost of site-built homes is prohibitive. They generally don't appreciate at rates similar to those of other types of homes, but the quality and size of today's models help to shed the stigma from years past.

As with any other home, when appraising these alterative types of construction, the appraiser is tasked with identifying local comps that match the type of the subject property. If you're looking for that amazing log cabin perched high in the mountains of Montana, keep in mind that financing it could be tough because finding similarly built log homes in the same wilderness area may be difficult. Without viable comparable sales comparisons, an accurate appraised value can be hard to identify. And lenders are sticklers for making sure that they are comfortable with the value of the home before they allow cash to rain into your bank account. Geodesic dome houses also share this headwind when trying to get a home loan. They are cool to live in, can stand up against wind and snow like the Jolly Green Giant, but are rare enough that finding another to do your "96 Corolla sales comparison" might be very difficult.

Inspections

Inspections often go hand in hand with appraisals. Though not always required by the lender, they are a smart investment for the homebuyer when considering the purchase of a pre-existing home (versus a new construction). Imagine you come across a beautiful red 1961 Ferrari GT250 California Spyder in some dude's garage and he wants to sell it after it was taken for a joyride through the streets of Chicago by his son's best friend. You walk around the car looking at it from every angle and kick all four tires before deciding it looks perfect. But you're smart. You decide to have a qualified inspector look over it before you make an offer to buy it out of the glass-walled garage. Good thing you did because the inspector finds that 80% of the car is covered in body filler to fill in the dents left by some idiot who launched it out the back of the garage into a ravine. The odometer has been tampered with, the motor has been overheated, warping the cylinder head and the gearbox has been ground so many times it should be registered with the Food and Drug Administration as a meat grinding facility. Someone slapped some lipstick on that pig and tried to sell it as "cherry." Houses can have the same lipstick treatment. A fresh coat of paint over rotting siding makes even the most dilapidated hunk of junk look good. It's hard to spot water leaks in the ceiling after a few cans of the local hardware store's best latex has been slathered on. Foundations can be cracked, sewer lines can be clogged and attics can be full of moisture due to improper ventilation. To the untrained eye, countless shortcomings may be overlooked. Scrutiny by a qualified inspector helps to identify problem areas that either need to be addressed or are deal killers. If you end up finding some issues, think carefully about what it will take to rectify them. And don't believe what you see on TV … a complete remodel cannot be done in 30 minutes with $2,000 and some elbow grease before the big reveal in front of you and all your family.

Chapter Eight

Flood zones

Whether you are buying a new home or refinancing your existing one, your lender will obtain a flood zone determination from their flood certificate vendor. The Federal Emergency Management Agency (FEMA) performs surveys to determine areas that may be affected by a flood at some point. They assign a letter to an area that corresponds with the likelihood that it may be subject to flooding under the right metrological circumstances. Flood zones are identified alphabetically with designations like X, B, C, A or V. Some do not have a high enough risk of flooding to warrant concern by the lender. Others will require the purchase of flood insurance through an appropriate provider. If you find yourself with a home in a flood zone that falls into this category, work with your lender to determine how much flood insurance you will need to satisfy the lending requirements and from whom you can obtain that insurance. Not all insurance companies offer the right kind of insurance. Also, be sure to shop around. Flood insurance premiums can vary widely from company to company. They can get expensive so be sure you have the right coverage that is cost effective and from a reputable company.

Mortgage insurance

We need to discuss mortgage insurance for a bit because—to be honest—it gets a bad rap. I can't count how many times I've had a customer tell me how much of a rip-off mortgage insurance is because they must pay for it every month and it only benefits the lender. It is true that mortgage insurance is beneficial to the lender if they have to file a claim because of borrower payment default, but the fact is that—without it—there is little or no chance that individual would have been granted a loan in the first place.

You'll learn shortly, when reading about "underwriting," that assessing the viability of mortgage loans is all about risk. Any given lending institution has a risk profile that loans must fall into. That certainly applies to mortgage loans, but it also applies to all others too like commercial and consumer loans (cars, boats, personal etc.). If characteristics of the loan do not fit the risk profile of the lender evaluating it, they will not approve the loan. Maybe the prospective borrower's credit history is not up to the standards the lender is looking for. Or the loan-to-value (LTV) is higher than they are comfortable with. There can be any number of reasons why someone may not approve a loan. Each lender has their own unique box that the loan characteristics must fit into if an approval is going to be made.

The LTV of a given loan has a big impact on approvals. Put yourself in the lender's shoes. If your friend, Buddy the elf, comes to you asking for a loan to buy a syrup factory, some of the first few questions you may ask are: How much money do you want to borrow? What is the sales price of the factory? What kind of down payment are you going to make? If Buddy tells you he is buying the syrup factory for one million dollars and he has no money for a down payment, then he is effectively asking you to make a loan at 100% LTV (the amount of the loan is 100% of the purchase price). You, being the risk-conscious person you are, realize that, if Buddy's syrup business plan fails and he is unable to make payments on the loan you made to him, you'd have to repossess the factory and hopefully sell it to someone else for at least the amount of the loan you had made on it, which is probably 100% of the value. If Buddy ate all the inventory and decorated all the equipment in a winter motif that no one wants to pay for, you may be stuck selling it for less than you put into it. Never mind the resources you expended to make the loan: Paying an underwriter to evaluate the risk, closers to draft the closing documents, etc. Most likely, you'd want Buddy to put some money down on the factory so that you are lending money at an acceptable percentage of its overall value. But how much do you require him to put down? And what if he does not have the cash available for your required minimum down payment? This is where mortgage insurance comes in to save the day.

In the home lending world, mortgage insurance will usually be required on loans where the LTV exceeds 80% (for conventional loans). Most lenders are comfortable making a loan where the customer puts at least 20% down because, in the event of a default, there is enough equity in the property so that, if it's taken back and sold, the lender can recover their investment in it. It is when the down payment is less than 20% (and the LTV is greater than 80%) that lenders start to get nervous. The chances are extremely good that a loan won't be approved if the LTV is above 80% unless the lender has something that mitigates the risk. Mortgage insurance is that risk mitigator. It gives the lender peace of mind because, if payments are not made on the loan, the lender can make a claim from the mortgage insurance company that ultimately reduces or eliminates their exposure above 80% LTV.

So, in our example, Buddy would not have been approved to get the loan without mortgage insurance. However, *with* mortgage insurance, he has to pay a little more each month in his mortgage payment to cover the cost of the insurance. But he gets the loan to purchase his syrup factory and he lives happily ever after.

Chapter Nine

Fulfillment

We have covered a lot so far. But we haven't even built the loan file yet or sent it to someone to make a decision on it. The real "meat and potatoes" of the mortgage loan process hasn't really begun at this point. The file must still be processed and underwritten (with the closing documents drawn up and then signed), funded, closed and shipped off to some investor. "Fulfillment" is mortgage vernacular for all these steps just mentioned. Another way of putting it is all the "back-office" work that has to be performed once the application has been completed and appropriate documentation has been obtained (recall the income and asset documentation we spoke of earlier). We'll discuss the fulfillment steps in the order that they generally occur, starting with processing.

Processing

A loan processor is *one of* the unsung heroes of mortgage lending. They are charged with "cleaning up" all the chaos that is often dropped on their desk by a loan officer. More often than not, a loan officer is very good at working with consumers to identify the right loan program details to suit the needs of their customers. They are sales-oriented folks who are generally not particularly adept at the details. And that is perfectly okay. They are good at what they do and arguably should stay in their lane. Processors are the detail-oriented magicians who wave their magic wand (in the form of a blue pen) to turn a pile of rubbish into a beautiful loan file ready for an underwriter to be wowed by.

Once you have completed the application and provided the documentation asked of you by your loan officer, the processor gets to work. They will take all those paystubs, bank statements, tax returns and anything else that has been collected and start to organize it. They make sure numbers match and blanks are filled so that they can paint the most accurate picture of you as a borrower to the decision makers (the underwriters). It is not at all uncommon for a processor to make a request for additional documentation after they have reviewed the file. Yeah, I know … you already went through a ton of effort to gather up enough paperwork to fill a dump truck and now you're being asked for another pickup load worth. Sorry about that. When setting up the file, it's normal for things to be identified that weren't previously known and call for additional information or documentation. An example might be a divorce. If during the analysis of your bank statements, it becomes obvious that each month sees the receipt (or payment) of alimony or child support, then you will be asked for a divorce decree to see what you may be obligated to pay or entitled to receive. Payment of child support or alimony will be counted as part of your liabilities like a car or student loan payment. If you are on the receiving end of that, then you get to use it as income, provided it will continue for at least another three years. If you have a new job, additional documentation may be necessary to qualify the income from that job. The list of things that could spur the call for more paperwork is endless. It is the duty of the processor to identify those missing items in the loan file to make sure that their masterpiece is painted in a complete manner for the underwriter. These requests for information or paperwork can be tedious, but please cut the processors some slack: They are trying very hard to identify everything necessary to approve the file with the goal of getting an approval on the loan the first time the underwriter sees it. It's a big ask, but the more you help the processor at this point, the smoother the trip across the finish line.

Underwriting

An underwriter analyzes risk. When doing that, they look at the four "C's" of underwriting, which have nothing to do with buying a diamond. In this case, the four C's are: Credit, Collateral, Capacity and Cash. By examining these four areas, underwriters attempt to determine the lender's risk of default by the borrower and, alternatively, the likelihood of repayment of the loan as agreed. Their talent lies in looking at the obvious and uncovering the not-so-obvious. My mother retired after 40+ years of mortgage underwriting. She was really good at identifying what was *not* said, which is extremely valuable for a lender's risk analysis but was horrible if you were a teenager trying to get away with something you shouldn't. As a homage to my mom, let's take a look at the four C's to figure out what they are looking for.

Chapter Ten

Credit

You've all seen the commercials on TV for services that help raise your credit score. In their own cinematic way, they describe how doors open and clouds part to let sunshine through when you have a higher credit score. Putting my own personal sentiments about these commercials aside, it's generally true that better credit does yield better loan terms. Mortgage loans, like many others are "risk based" in that the higher the risk of a given loan, the higher the cost of borrowing. "Higher borrowing cost" generally manifests itself through higher interest rates (see the "interest rate" section). Your credit history helps identify your dedication to paying your bills as agreed. If you have a long history of paying on time, you can expect your credit score to reflect this by being higher than those who do not. Paying on time isn't the only factor though. The number of open accounts and length of time they have been open plays into it as well. You may have made all your car payments on time but, if you have only had the car loan for three months, this does not paint a historical picture. Underwriters want to see that you not just pay on time but have done so for a long time, thus indicating a trend of responsible use of credit. The number of tradelines (fancy word for a credit account) is important too. If you have too few, there isn't enough data to create a complete credit picture. If you have too many or the ones you have are maxed out, it may indicate too much use of credit. What is the magic formula for a great credit score? It's hard to say. I've been looking at credit reports for almost 30 years and I still don't know. If you ask five "experts" on the subject, you'll probably get five different answers with three of them being somewhat similar. If I were doling out advice (take it for what it is worth), I'd suggest three to five tradelines with at least one year's worth of on-time payments. That will set you well on your way to a credit profile that an underwriter likes.

While we are on the subject of credit, a word to the wise: Don't go out and make any significant purchases while navigating the mortgage loan process. Many people seem to think that, after the initial credit report is pulled (usually at the beginning of the process), they are free to go buy whatever they want without consequences. People will buy furniture for the new house and a truck to haul it home in without realizing that a pre-close credit "refresh" happens a few days before the closing table to verify that no new tradelines have been opened and the balances on the existing ones are largely unchanged. I have personally witnessed hundreds of wonderful people fail to close their loan because they no longer qualify after buying something they couldn't wait another two weeks for. So, please, for your sake and that of your lender, leave the credit card in the wallet and pull out the Benjamins instead (if retail therapy is absolutely necessary).

Collateral

Just like "tradeline" is a fancy word for a credit account, "collateral" is a fancy word for the home you are financing. When an unsecured loan is made to a person or entity, the lender has not taken something of value as collateral on the loan. Mortgage loans are not unsecured. They use the house and property as collateral so that, if the loan is not paid back as agreed, the lender has the opportunity to take back that home in order to recover their investment. So, when the underwriter looks at the collateral portion of the home loan, they review the appraisal. I mentioned in the "appraisal" section the abundance of information collected on a home when an appraiser writes up an appraisal report. The underwriter will review it all. Things like condition of the home, age, size, room count, neighborhood and value trends in the area are just small parts of what is taken into account when they determine if the home (and accompanying land) is adequate collateral for the loan. Imagine a dilapidated cabin in the woods on half an acre that is 350 square feet in size, a cot next to a single pane window, a wood stove with a cool old enamel tea kettle on top whistling the tune of boiling water and an outhouse 30 yards from the back door. It's quaint and appealing to those who are looking for simplicity and remote living, but the chances that a lender is going to approve a loan of $1 million (read in the voice of Dr. Evil) are relatively slim. The

65

property is probably not worth that and the condition of the cabin isn't conducive to a quality home built to last 30+ years. That is an extreme example. However, it illustrates the idea that an underwriter is looking to the appraisal to make sure that the home being put up as collateral has a value and condition commensurate with the loan being taken out against it.

Capacity

When I think of capacity, I usually think of the amount that something can hold— like "the capacity of my fuel tank makes it painful when I fill up at the pump." In the mortgage context, "capacity" has to do with the amount that someone can afford on a monthly basis to repay the loan. There are three major factors when determining someone's capacity to repay a loan: 1. Income, 2. Expenses (aka "liabilities") and 3. Debt ratio as calculated by #1 and #2. We discussed in the "Income" section that, once a lender determines your gross monthly income, they shoot for about 43% of that being allocated to all monthly expenses (including your new mortgage). Expenses and liabilities are the monthly payments you're obligated to, usually shown on your credit report as well as any undisclosed loan debt you may have. The percentage of income to expenses is what produces the debt ratio that underwriters look at when rendering a decision. That analysis goes hand in hand with the underwriter determining the capacity of the borrower(s) to repay the loan. If the debt ratio exceeds the lender's maximum for a given loan program, then the applicant(s) don't have the capacity to repay the loan. One of three things can occur to help someone's capacity to repay: 1. Increase gross monthly income, 2. Reduce monthly expenses and 3. Reduce the loan amount being applied for.

Cash

Ahhhh, the almighty dollar. The late Notorious B.I.G. taught us that with mo[re] money come mo[re] problems. I have no doubt there is validity to that, but I also believe that there are inherent problems when there is not enough cash on hand as well. An example of not having enough available greenbacks is the inability to produce an adequate down payment to get approved for a loan. We noted a couple of loan programs that have a zero down-payment option, but, outside of those rare circumstances, we generally need a down payment when purchasing a home. We also need funds to be able to pay the closing costs associated with the loan. With this in mind, underwriters will look at an applicant's available cash to determine if it's enough to approve the loan. This is most often done by looking at bank statements or some other form of verification of money deposited into a financial institution. Checking and savings accounts, investment accounts and even sometimes cryptocurrency are considered when analyzing someone's cash position.

Chapter Eleven

Closing

The end goal of any loan transaction (mortgage or otherwise) is closing. This is when all parties involved sign the legal and regulatory documents before funds can be disbursed to whomever appropriate. It's also a very complex step in the process where attention to detail is paramount. Home loans have a lot of critical parts. Chief among them are the Note (which is the IOU part of the loan) and the security instrument (usually a Deed of Trust or Mortgage). If these documents are not drafted perfectly and recorded appropriately with the correct municipality (generally the county where the property is located), the lender can lose their right to foreclose and/or repossess the property in the event of non-payment of the loan. The documents are lengthy, complex and designed by an attorney to protect both the consumer and the lender. The typical chronological steps in the closing process are as follows:

1. Drafting all the closing documents and sending them to the closing agent. This step is completed by the closing department of your lender.
2. The closing agent reviews all the documents and settlement statement to verify accuracy.

3. All parties involved sign the documents, often at the title company or by engaging a notary at a location convenient to you.
4. The lender receives the signed documents back from the closing agent and reviews them for accuracy.
5. Disbursement of funds as appropriate.
6. Recording of the security instrument.

The good news for you is that basically all the complexity of this part of getting a home loan is done behind the scenes. Your lender and settlement agent(s) handle it. The extent of your involvement is limited to signing a stack of documents that resemble a ream of paper at the closing table and bringing certified funds to the closing table (if necessary). There are a lot of pages and there is a very high likelihood that you could develop writer's cramp by the time you're the proud new owner of a home (or, in the case of a refinance, the owner of a new debt obligation on your existing home). Often this process happens pretty efficiently (in a few days), but sometimes it can take a little longer. Your lender will work hard to complete these steps no later than your contracted close date but be sure to give them some time to check that everything is done perfectly. An "i" not dotted or a "t" not crossed can have big ramifications for all involved.

Settlement agents

Settlement agents are third-party companies that help with the closing of a loan. Common settlement service providers include title companies, escrow companies and closing attorneys. They each serve different purposes and can even be found in different parts of the county, but they all contribute in their own ways toward the same end goal: Closing out your loan transaction and all that entails. For example, closing attorneys are more likely to be found east of the Mississippi River whereas escrow companies can be accessed by crossing the bank to the west shore all the way to the Pacific coast. As with everything, there are exceptions to that and somewhere in the middle of the country there begins a transition from one to another. Each performs a very important role in their own way.

Title companies will perform a title search and also provide title insurance. To better understand this, let's recall our cream puff 1996 Toyota Corolla. Once you've found the perfect one to buy, you will most likely want to know if it has a "clear title," meaning that it's free from any liens and not "branded" due to something like a wreck or GTA-style theft by a 13-year-old taking it on a joyride through the 'burbs. If the seller of the car has a loan against it, that loan must be paid off and the lien removed from the title before you can have the title transferred to your name. Houses are similar. Liens can be filed against the home by contractors (oddly called "mechanics liens"), lenders, homeowners' associations (for non-payment of dues), ex-spouses for child or spousal support, governments for non-payments of taxes or anyone else who feels they have a claim against the home or homeowner. On your mission to own the home, you'll want to be cognizant of any abnormalities in the title. For that, we have our friends at title companies who perform a search of the local county records to make sure that everything is copacetic. If they find a lien or some other problem, they will alert your loan officer and set them on a path to address the issue(s). Once anything that needs resolution is taken care of, they will issue a clear title and title insurance. Why the heck does anyone need that? It's simple … you [will have] paid for the research on it and you will want assurances that the work they did was thorough and accurate. Should a lien or something pop up on title at some point down the road based on an event that predates the title search, that title insurance ensures that it's the title company's problem to resolve, not yours. Having recently purchased a pickup from an unscrupulous seller that ended up having all kinds of issues that should have led to a branded title, I can attest to the importance of title insurance on a home (something that costs way more than my pickup). There are two different types of title insurance you'll see in your closing documents: Owners' title insurance and lenders' title insurance. They perform essentially the same function. However, one protects your lender (hence the name) and the other protects you. In some states, owners' title insurance is optional, but lenders' title insurance will be required by your lender. In the grand scheme of things, it's relatively inexpensive and, should it ever be needed, you'll be glad you have it. Liens on a property can be tens of thousands or even hundreds of thousands of dollars. No one wants to write that check due to an error having been made during the title search process.

In addition to making sure that the title to your new home is all good, title companies will also make sure that all appropriate documents are recorded and on file with the local municipality (usually the county courthouse). In some cases, that requires a trip down to the courthouse to talk with the clerk behind the desk possibly wearing the green visor and stamping documents with great vengeance and furious anger. In other cases, it's possible to record documents electronically. It just depends on how technologically advanced the local county courthouse's records division is.

Escrow

Escrow companies are another of our settlement provider friends. Let's say you've been searching the world wide web for the absolutely perfect metallic mint green 1963 Pontiac Tempest because it had the same body length, height, width, wheel base and track of the '64 Buick Skylark, except that it came with a limited slip differential. Now you want this car badly because it can lay rubber with *both* rear wheels outside the Sack-O-Suds—so, when you find it, you don't want to let it go. After talking with the seller, he tells you he's had three other calls on it while talking to you. You work out a deal whereby you send him $500 as a deposit while you get your financing ironed out and buy a plane ticket to Alabama. But you're smart: You don't give the seller the $500 directly, possibly enabling him to keep it and sell the car to some lady named Ms. Mona Lisa Vito. Instead, you find a disinterested third party whose business is to hold the $500 for you and the seller until such time as the transaction is finalized and then release it to the seller with your say-so. If the deal falls through, you get your $500 back without fear of the seller keeping it (provided that was the deal you made) and the seller sleeps well at night knowing that there is a legitimate $500 out there with his name on it instead of the buyers saying, "The check is in the mail, bro." This disinterested third party is an escrow company. These hold the "earnest money" that a home buyer pledges to the seller as a way of saying, "Hey man, I'm serious about buying your pad. Here's some sweet moolah to prove that I'm serious while I work with my awesome loan officer to secure financing." The amount of the earnest money and the terms surrounding it will be detailed in the purchase and sale contract that is signed by the buyer and the seller. Word of caution: Some of these contracts can be written in a way that causes the seller of the home to keep the earnest money even if the sale does not go through. Work with your real estate agent or attorney to make sure that the terms of the contract are favorable to all involved.

Closing attorneys perform duties similar to title companies. It can be easy to confuse these folks with real estate attorneys. They are often the same people. However, they perform duties in a different manner. A real estate attorney is who you seek help from when you have a legal dispute of some kind. As a closing attorney, they help with title searches, insurance and document recording. The other notable difference can be found with the title work. A title company will issue a "title commitment" whereas a closing attorney will issue a "title abstract." They serve the same purpose and, to a consumer, they are no different from one another.

Chapter Twelve

Servicing

If you've left the closing table after having signed your name enough times to run the inkwell dry, then the chances are that you have either been given the keys to your new home or you have a new mortgage with a [hopefully] lower rate on your existing home and maybe even some cash in hand to do with as you like. Congratulations. That's a huge milestone. Simultaneous to your reaching the end of the process, a new widget has been born: A mortgage loan. And, like any newborn, it requires nurturing and constant attention and monitoring, as it grows up to be a fully mature loan. If you have offspring of your own, you know how much work this can be. Heck, if you have a pet that you have had since it came home as a baby, you're well aware of the effort that goes into keeping something alive, healthy and performing as it should throughout its life. Mortgage loans are no different, albeit that they tend to leave fewer messes on the carpet and don't require a diaper bag to be toted around like an adult binky. For this potentially 30-year-long task, we call upon the Mortgage Loan Servicing Department of the lender (or the successor and/or assigned entity identified to perform this duty). A loan servicer is tasked with a number of duties that are too numerous to detail in this publication. Like appraisals, an entire book could be dedicated to the topic of mortgage loan servicing alone. We will narrow the scope of what they do down to those things that may have a direct impact on you as the homeowner.

It has been said that there are two things certain in life: Death and taxes. I *really* hope your mortgage loan has nothing to do with death. Taxes, however, are another matter. Unless you have some sort of special deal made with the county assessor's office, the chances are that you have to pay property taxes on your home. Throughout the course of getting a loan, you may have been asked by your loan officer if you'd like to pay your property taxes yourself (possible under certain circumstances) when they are due or have your lender pay them for you: The same goes with your homeowner's insurance. If you choose to have your lender pay it on your behalf, then they will set up an escrow account whereby a portion of your monthly mortgage payment is deposited to be used later to pay taxes and insurance. Let's keep the math simple for an example: Your annual property taxes amount to $1,200 and the annual premium for your homeowner's insurance policy comes to $600. That's $1,800 worth of checks that have to be written each year. If you have your taxes and insurance "escrowed," (aka "impounded"), then, each month you make your mortgage payment, $150 of it will be deposited into the account that is earmarked to pay these items. It's commonly called the "impounds" account. By doing this, your lender will write the $1,200 check to the county for you when the time is right, as they will for the $600 homeowners' insurance premium. Seems simple, right? Well, on your loan, it is. But keep in mind that a mortgage loan servicing department or company may have tens of thousands of loans in their portfolio that they are required to perform this service on. That's a lot of checks to write, funds to manage, property tax bills to keep track of and insurance premiums to ensure get paid. It's a very complex machine to keep well-oiled and running smoothly. And that is just one small part of what they do. All these loans they are charged with managing make payments monthly, sometimes bi-monthly. Those payments have to be received, property documented and accounted for. Receiving those payments isn't as simple as it seems. In the old days, they arrived in the mail in the form of a check with a payment coupon. Today, they arrive via electronic funds transfers, online bill payments, checks and even cash at the teller window of a bank. Regardless of how the money comes flying in the door, it all has to be accounted for down to the penny. Then the loan servicing team has to properly allocate it. As mentioned earlier under "The fixed-rate mortgage" section, the average mortgage payment has four components to it: Principal, interest, taxes and insurance. The principal and interest (P&I) portions of the payment often go to an investor who bought the rights to collect those portions of the payment. When, how and where the P&I portions go can differ for every one of those loans. The tax and insurance portions must be properly allocated to the aforementioned impound account where they sit and wait to be sent to the county and insurance company when called for. Maybe you are financially responsible and ambitious and make additional payments to the principal to help get your loan paid down more quickly. The accounting on those payments is different from standard minimum payments and can require special attention.

Servicing teams attend to other needs as well. If your house elf was feeling naughty and decided to create a hurricane in the middle of your house, drenching everything you own in a torrential downpour before blowing it all to the Leaky Cauldron, then you probably will have lost all your loan-related documents. If you want a copy of them to put in your new elf-proof enchanted file cabinet, you can call your servicing friends to send you copies of those documents. Similarly, maybe your mean Uncle Vernon Dursley has been intercepting all your outgoing and incoming mail so that your mortgage payments never made it to the lender and the notices to pay weren't put on your desk. It is the job of the servicing department to engage in loss-mitigation practices. Believe it or not, no one wants to foreclose on your house. It's an incredibly long, expensive and horrible process to repossess a home. NO ONE and I do mean NO ONE, wants to do that. They would rather just get their monthly mortgage payment and everyone be happy. But, if that does not happen, we have what is called "loss mitigation" (commonly called "loss-mit"). Loss-mit is simply trying to mitigate the loss to the lender and homeowner. If payments aren't made as agreed, then the loss-mit department will attempt to connect with the homeowner to find a reasonable solution to the problem. Maybe the homeowner got injured and can't work for a couple of months while they recover. In that case, it might be possible to reduce payments for that time until they are able to go back to work. Or maybe refinancing the home to lower the monthly payment is an option, making it easier for the homeowner to make that payment. Keep in mind that none of these "mitigation options" are guaranteed. However, it is in the best interest of the lender to find a way to get the homeowner back on track to on-time payments as agreed: It benefits the lender and, more importantly, it benefits the owner of the home. If you've had a hardship that resulted in payments not being made as they should, don't dodge the phone calls from the loan servicing department. They genuinely want to help if they can.

Your loan servicer will try hard to make sure that the experience you have when contacting them is a good one. This is especially true when the servicer is a financial institution that wants to keep your business. The chances are that you will one day want to refinance your mortgage or buy a new home. They hope your experience as a customer is good enough so, when that time comes, you go back to them for that refinance or new home purchase.

Up to this point, we've covered a fraction of what the servicing folks do. It's complicated, arduous and laden with opportunities to make a mistake. So why would anyone want to do it? Well, believe it or not, people actually pay for the opportunity to service mortgage loans (they are called "Mortgage Servicing Rights" or "MSR's"). Remember we referred to a mortgage loan as a "widget," and that a widget can be bought and sold as with any other commodity? The servicing of a loan is one of the components of a mortgage loan that is bought and sold by people who want the rights to do all that work. It's very possible that, once your loan is closed, you'll end up getting a notice in the mail saying your loan has been sold. Or that the servicing of your loan has been transferred. Or both. The Note (the IOU part of the loan where you promise to pay it all back) can be sold to an investor, giving them the rights to collect the P&I portions of your loan payment. The servicing of that loan can also be sold. There is a massive industry out there that involves the monthly processing of mortgage payments. These companies that specialize in loan servicing get paid handsomely for performing these services. As you may imagine, servicing one or two loans isn't profitable or practical. But, with economies of scale in play, companies can make a decent living by servicing hundreds of thousands or even millions of loans each month. If you have the right software, people and understanding of how it works, you can do it well and profitably on a large scale. It's rare that anyone *wants* their loan or servicing sold. So how do you determine if it will be? There is no guarantee that it will or won't be. However, you'd be smart to ask your loan officer if they generally sell or retain their loans once closed. It's not uncommon for community banks to retain the servicing of their loans to help keep their customers happy.

Chapter Thirteen

Quality assurance and quality control

Quality assurance (QA) and quality control (QC) are two internal procedures that most consumers would know nothing about. If done correctly, they are transparent to the homeowner. However, things happen, so we are going to talk about how QA and/or QC could have an impact on you both during and after the loan process. First, let's talk about the differences between them. QA and QC are designed to perform similar functions—Both look for errors in the loan origination process. Those errors could have to do with procedures that weren't followed, regulations that weren't adhered to or documents that may be missing. QA and QC are required by investors and regulators to be completed on roughly 10% of mortgage loans. The biggest difference between them is that QA functions are performed before the close of a loan whereas QC activities are done post-close.

The QA portion is what could have an impact on your loan process. Lenders are usually required to run about 10% of their in-process loan files through the QA department. This is often done after final approval is given and before the closing documents are drawn up. The process could take between three hours and three days. Files are chosen at random and the QA staff must be given time to do their work. That could unexpectedly delay your loan closing by a day or so. It may also give rise to additional items needed before going to closing. Based on the frequency of loans being chosen for QA review, the likelihood that you will be affected by it is slim, but it happens.

QC is a different beast. It happens post-close and will most likely result in third-party verifications being performed on things like your employment and/or income. One of the goals of QC reviews is to verify that the lender has not falsified any documentation with the intent of closing the loan when it would otherwise not be qualified. The chances are you will never know that this is occurring. However, in some rare cases, the third-party verification company may call your supervisor or human resources department to verify your employment and they may in turn alert you to someone asking questions. This is normal. Rare, but normal. Don't be alarmed if it happens. But, if it does, I think the best advice would be to contact your loan officer and verify that a third party is performing this federally mandated QC measure.

Delays due to quality checks can be frustrating. However, they are done with the best of intentions— to make sure that the consumer (you) is being taken care of correctly and without bias.

Chapter Fourteen

Conclusion

Well, there you have it: The mortgage loan process in a nutshell. It is complex, time-consuming and burdensome, even on a good day. However, it provides several different options for consumers to realize the American dream of home ownership. Like the disclaimers found at the end of the commercials for some new pharmaceutical, I leave you with this: Each step of the process discussed in this book is simplified. It's also just one way of doing it and there is certainly more than one "right way" to originate a mortgage loan. As the financial crisis of 2008 showed us, there are definitely *wrong* ways to do it as well. Your personal experience in getting a home loan will vary from that of your friends and neighbors. Each loan officer has their own unique customer service experience—as do different lending companies. It is what allows them to create their own individual brands. The basics are covered here but you can expect some derivation one way or another from what you have read.

I hope this has given you some semblance of understanding of what is happening beyond what you discuss with your loan officer. That understanding can make it easier to anticipate and navigate the process, especially as it can be drawn out over several weeks.

Thanks for devoting some time to reading through this. One of the best parts of my job is working with customers who are prepared and educated about mortgage lending. Count yourself among that select group!

Glossary

Annual Percentage Rate (APR)

The APR represents the true cost of the loan if it is taken to the full term (meaning not paid off early). Its purpose is to help in comparing one lender with another by giving a more "apples-to-apples" comparison versus interest rate alone.

Borrower

The "borrower" is the industry term for a consumer who has become a customer. If you as a consumer decide to do business with a loan officer named Bartholomew J. Simpson, then Mr. Simpson may refer to you as the "borrower" while discussing the loan file internally.

Broker

A broker is a loan originator who does not work for a bank or an IMB but will help a customer complete a loan application and gather all required documentation for a third-party lending institution to underwrite and close the loan. That third party is called a wholesaler and the broker acts as an intermediary between the customer/borrower and the wholesale lender.

Conforming loan

No, this is not a utopian society thing where everyone looks the same. A conforming loan is eligible for purchase by Freddie Mac and/or Fannie Mae and is at or under the conforming loan limit. The conforming loan limit can change annually depending on market conditions. To determine what the current limit is, perform an internet search for "conforming loan limit" and make sure you're looking at the current calendar year when presented with the loan limit. In some "high cost" areas (such as major metropolitan areas), you may have what is called a "super conforming" loan limit, which will exceed the conforming loan limit but may be sold to Fannie and Freddie without being classified as a "jumbo" loan.

Debt ratio a.k.a. debt to income ratio (DTI)
DTI is one of the three main ratios that lenders use when qualifying a customer for a home loan. It is a representation of your total monthly expenses compared with your total gross monthly income. To simplify things, if your total monthly gross income is $10,000 and the total of all your monthly obligations (which include your proposed new mortgage payment, car payments, credit card payments, student loans, etc.) is $4,300, then your DTI is 43%. There are different DTI maximums for qualification purposes depending on the lender, loan program and the purpose of your loan. However, it's safe to shoot for about a 43% DTI when evaluating how much you can qualify for.

Department of Veterans Affairs (VA)
The VA does *a lot* for those who have served our country. For the purposes of what we are covering here, we will limit our discussion to their contributions to home ownership. The VA provides a guarantee to

lending institutions against payment default on their loan products. These loan products are only available to qualified individuals who served or are currently serving in our country's armed forces. Very generally, active duty or retired members of our military can receive VA benefits to purchase a home as long as they were not "other than honorably" discharged. In some cases, these benefits may be available to a non-military spouse as well.

Fannie Mae (FNMA)

The Federal National Mortgage Association is one of the two more commonly known government-sponsored enterprises (GSEs) that are charged with providing liquidity to the secondary mortgage market and providing guarantees to investors of mortgage-backed securities (MBS). They provide the liquidity by buying closed mortgage loans from origination companies (such as banks or independent mortgage bankers) so they do not have to leave the loans "on their books," thus retaining liquidity to provide more mortgage loans to more consumers. These loans ultimately get securitized into Mortgage Backed Securities (MBS), which in turn get sold to investors. When the investors buy them, they do so with the confidence that comes from Fannie Mae guaranteeing the payment of principal and interest to the investor, even in the event of non-payment by the borrower who obtained the loan. The nature and scope of that guarantee can vary depending on the product type and lender.

Federal Home Loan Bank (FHLB)

There are 11 government-sponsored Federal Home Loan Banks around the country that provide access to liquidity for member financial institutions, generally on a short-term basis (such as overnight). They are the third government-sponsored enterprise (GSE) along with , Fannie Mae and Freddie Mac. Many mortgage industry professionals are unaware that FHLB is a GSE.

Federal Housing Administration (FHA)
The FHA is part of the Department of Housing and Urban Development (HUD). It provides insurance to mortgage lenders against losses when a payment default occurs on a loan they have insured. FHA programs help facilitate access to mortgage financing for low-to-moderate-income individuals. They also have programs designed to help first-time homebuyers obtain financing to purchase their first home.

Federal Housing Finance Agency (FHFA)
The FHFA is kind of like the parent for Freddie, Fannie and the FHLBs. It regulates, supervises and provides oversight of the GSEs. It came to be as a result of some legislation passed in 2008 in the wake of the financial crisis.

Freddie Mac (FHLMC)
The Federal Home Loan Mortgage Corporation is the other of the two most commonly known GSEs. For simplicity's sake, we will say that Freddie is essentially the same as Fannie. Despite being two separate entities, they operate in a very similar manner with the same goals.

Independent Mortgage Bank (IMB)

IMBs are mortgage banking companies that are not part of a bank. They work as independent lenders rather than depository institutions. They offer many of the same or similar mortgage loan products as most banks. However, they do not work under the supervision of a depository institution.

Interest rate

This is what most people are focused on. It's what guys brag about at the bar with their buddies to see who has the lowest rate on their mortgage. It's the interest rate found on the Note: the cost of borrowing money from the lending institution because—let's face it—you don't get to borrow money for free. If you borrow $100,000, you're going to have to pay it back with interest. The rate at which the interest accrues on an annual basis is referred to as the Note rate or the interest rate. From a consumer standpoint, the lower the better. From an investor standpoint, the higher the better. The going market rate is somewhere between those two.

Jumbo loan

When you exceed the conforming loan limit, you're now in "jumbo" territory. A jumbo loan is any mortgage loan that exceeds the conforming loan limit (if even by a penny). These loans are ineligible for delivery to the GSEs and are generally sold to private (non-government-sponsored) investors (such as large banks).

Lender

This term can be confusing. Depending on who you ask and what part of the county you're in, a "lender" can be a term synonymous with "loan officer" or it can refer to the lending institution that a loan officer works for. For example, a loan officer named Billy Ray Valentine may work for a lender, Duke & Duke. However, management within Duke & Duke may refer to Mr. Valentine as their mortgage lender. Listen to the context in which the term "lender" is used. If it is referring to a company, then understand that they are talking about the lending institution the loan officer works for.

Loan officer

Despite what some people think, the loan officer who works with you to obtain a mortgage loan is not some random person who decides to stop selling cars on Monday and do loans on Tuesday. A mortgage loan officer (MLO) is required to complete annual training and, in some cases, pass a state and federal exam before they can legally originate mortgage loans on behalf of a consumer. They must also be registered through the Nationwide Multistate Licensing System and Registry (NMLS). You can learn about your loan officer by accessing www.nmlsconsumeraccess.org and entering their name and/or NMLS registration number (required on all marketing they put out). Loan officers have been trained to navigate the multitude of hoops one must jump through to complete a mortgage loan. You'd be well advised to do your homework before deciding on a loan officer to work with. Ask friends and family for recommendations. Good ones make their living based on referrals from satisfied past clients.

Loan to value (LTV)

This is one of the other ratios that play an important role in qualifying for a loan. It's the ratio between the value of the home and the loan amount you are applying for. On a purchase transaction, the lesser of the purchase price or the appraised value will be compared against the loan amount. On a refinance, it is the appraised value against the loan amount. As an example, if you are purchasing a home for $400,000 (which is also the appraised value) and you're putting $80,000 down for a loan amount of $320,000, then your loan to value is 80% ($320k ÷ $400k = .80 or 80%).

Mortgage/Deed of Trust

A Mortgage and a Deed of Trust are two different documents, but they serve largely the same purpose. Each of them, in their own special way, create a security interest in the home that can be used by the lending institution to start foreclosure proceedings should they need to in the event of non-payment of the loan. The Note is the "I Owe You" (IOU) that says you'll pay back the loan. If you don't make those payments, the Mortgage or Deed of Trust is the legal document that allows the lender to take action … something the Note does not do on its own. Each state will generally favor either a Mortgage *or* a Deed of Trust. However, it is possible that both can be used within the same state.

Note

The Promissory Note is basically the IOU. It's a legal document that says the lending institution agrees to lend you "X" amount of money and in return you agree to pay it back over "Y" many months at "Z" interest rate.

Occupancy

What do you intend to use the home for: Primary residence, second (vacation) home or an investment property (a rental)? The occupancy type will impact how it is underwritten and what kinds of things you'll be asked to provide. For instance, on an investment property, you may be asked for six months' reserves … meaning you will have to show you have six-months' worth of mortgage payments in reserve in the event that the property is vacant for a while. That requirement is not always present on a primary residence. Pricing on your interest rate will also be impacted by the occupancy type. Generally, you'll find that interest rates are higher on second homes and investment properties compared with primary residences.

Overlay

An overlay is a requirement the lender has placed on a loan program that is over and above what is required by the investor. They are generally the result of an abundance of caution or because the risk appetite of the lender is a bit more conservative than that of the investor. For example, if the investor requires a minimum credit score of 600 for their loan product, but the lender who is offering that product to the consumer feels that a 600 credit score is too risky, they may require a minimum score of 620 in order to qualify with them.

Pre-Paid items ("Prepaids" for short)
Some items are required to be pre-paid at closing. The two most common prepaids are property taxes and homeowners' insurance. Those both must be paid one year in advance by the time the loan closes. Generally, those are paid as part of the loan closing but in some circumstances the [soon to be] homeowner can pay them in advance of closing as long as proof of payment can be provided. There can be exceptions to this rule but they are rare, so it's best to discuss with your loan officer.

Rate lock
Just like it sounds, a rate lock is how you "lock" in your rate to protect yourself against changing market conditions. Depending on volatility on any one given day, interest rates can fluctuate minute by minute. By locking it in, you have preserved your interest rate for a predetermined amount of time (often 30–90 days) irrespective of fluctuations in the mortgage market. Interest rates, just like any other widget (like a car) have a price associated with them.

Rural Development (RD) loans
The U.S. Department of Agriculture (USDA) provides loan programs aimed at rural areas where some investors are uncomfortable lending. They have solutions for properties on larger acreages as well as

zero-down programs for qualified individuals and properties.

Wholesaler

A wholesale lender is often a bank that will buy closed loans from mortgage brokers. They will underwrite, close and fund the loan that the broker originates, but they do not have any contact with the borrower directly during the origination process.

About the Author

Ron Culver began his career in mortgage lending in 1995 while working through college. Since then, he has endeavored to work in almost every capacity of the industry to further his understanding and knowledge of the business. He is a Certified Mortgage Banker and an Accredited Mortgage Professional, designations by the Mortgage Bankers Association that afforded him the opportunity to move into an educational capacity teaching other mortgage professionals and consumers alike about all aspects of mortgage lending.

www.ingramcontent.com/pod-product-compliance
Lightning Source LLC
Chambersburg PA
CBHW051231160726
47994CB00002B/841